Subscription the the English Church

(1st edition)

C. N. Wodehouse

Alpha Editions

This edition published in 2024

ISBN : 9789364733083

Design and Setting By
Alpha Editions
www.alphaedis.com
Email - info@alphaedis.com

As per information held with us this book is in Public Domain.
This book is a reproduction of an important historical work. Alpha Editions uses the best technology to reproduce historical work in the same manner it was first published to preserve its original nature. Any marks or number seen are left intentionally to preserve its true form.

SUBSCRIPTION
THE DISGRACE OF THE ENGLISH CHURCH.

IN human affairs, when attention is powerfully attracted to some question of absorbing interest, the effect frequently is as though one half only of the subject were visible to the eyes of the understanding. The mind fixes on some peculiar point. On that a partial light is exclusively cast; till in time it is discovered that others, consigned for a while to an unnatural obscurity, are in reality of greater moment. They have quietly grown in importance—like hardy trees unnoticed by the planter, as not requiring his care—till they are suddenly developed in their true character and vigour, to the astonishment of those who had overlooked them; and demand, if it be not too late, the deepest attention and the most active intelligence to control or direct them.

While Charles I. and Archbishop Laud were absorbed in maturing their favoured plans for Church and State, opposite and deeply-rooted opinions, whose force they never paused to appreciate till it was useless, were ripening all around them; and their lives became a sacrifice to their blindness. While James II. was only intent upon enforcing the dictates of his own one-eyed bigotry, the Revolution was already accomplished in the hearts of his people; and William III., the instrument to realize their wish, was almost at the gates of London. While Mr. Canning was delighting the electors of Liverpool with his eloquent, and to them convincing, denunciations against the minutest change in the parliamentary representation of this nation; while he was admonishing them, with a wisdom then esteemed oracular, "*Spartam nactus es, hanc adorna*," a few brief years were to give us almost a new Sparta; new electoral departments; new laws and forms of election; new qualifications, and thus new constituents; and, more than all, new influences upon electors and the representatives elected.

And thus, as it appears to the writer, will it come to pass with respect to the subject now to be briefly considered. While the minds of the most able divines in our nation are bent to one point; are engrossed in discussing the meaning of our Confession of Faith, the interpretation of our Articles of Religion; they are imperceptibly nourishing the growth of a conclusion more irresistible and more unmanageable than even all the complicated questions now so eagerly debated: for they are, by their differences and divisions, demolishing the whole force of the solemn assent required to that confession. Amidst the present confusion of tongues, the language of our Articles has still less than it ever had a definite meaning. Subscription, instead of being the tie which is to bind people to certain opinions or truths, is become a rope of sand. So uncertain is the trumpet's sound, that it no longer, as of old, proclaims the spirit of an united host, but turns every man's sword against his fellow: and Englishmen must soon awake to the conviction that Subscription, according to the plain meaning of words, is blown to the winds, and become the disgrace and not the safeguard of the English Church.

2. When the Saviour of mankind was about to leave this earth, He consoled his dejected followers with the promise of a gift which should even compensate for His loss, and exercise a special influence upon Christians in all future ages of this world's existence. "If I go not away the Comforter will not come." And He then announced one of the purposes for which He should come. "He shall guide you into all truth." Of all the qualities which can elevate the character and enlarge the usefulness of man, truth is the most lovely and powerful. If it be asked, what is, in briefest terms, the occupation of the ministers of Christ, it is, to exhibit truth to their people: and, in all their teaching, this it is which will establish their influence over the human heart, or at least that without which no wholesome influence can be exerted, namely, that each is a lover of truth.

But how is truth to be conveyed from man to man? Only through the medium of language. And what is language? A set of signs, or sounds, or words, which by general use and agreement mean certain things. But all human provisions are imperfect, and language is imperfect: and words may be artfully put together so as to have one meaning with the speaker, and another to the hearer; or written language may be twisted from its primary sense, and forced to a use contrary to the intention of the writer. Yet truth is a real thing, and every honest man knows that it is so; for whoever speaks that to another which he knows is not understood in his own sense by the hearer; whoever twists written language from the plain purpose of the writer; whoever, by a studied obscurity, veils his real opinions in order to mislead others, is a liar. Let no one be offended by a plain term which Scripture sanctions.

He who is justly branded with the imputation of such a vice as falsehood, is, in the common estimation of the best part of society, contemptible. But if a minister of the Gospel, a divinely commissioned teacher of truth, shall expose himself to such an imputation; if, in so solemn an act as Subscription to Articles of Faith, or in the interpretation of them, the plain meaning of words is evaded, or a sense put upon them which in common discourse between man and man would be deemed dishonourable and wicked, the character of that person as a teacher of truth must be damaged, and his influence impaired. He may indeed be surrounded by a set of admirers captivated by his talents, and their applauses may preserve his self-complacency, but the final verdict will yet be against him. It is possible that this error of the mind may arise from self-delusion, and then the guilt is diminished, but an evil result must still ensue; for as the root is so will be the plant, and good fruit cannot grow out of falsehood or dissimulation. If we remove the case from one individual to numbers, the general effect will of course be proportionably worse, and the conclusion will be drawn that *many* of the appointed teachers of truth are not lovers of truth.

We may take, however, a less extreme case, and suppose only, that amongst the teachers of truth a great difference of opinion has arisen as to some of the doctrines of which they are called upon to treat, as to the Confession of Faith which they have to maintain, and as to the terms of the Subscription by which they declare their assent to it. Then the conclusion will be—*when this difference is brought in glaring colours before the public eye*—either, that the Confession itself, or the form of assent, is so obscurely worded that it cannot be understood; or that they are intolerable to the conscience of many subscribers, and so must be somehow evaded; or lastly, that words, to which a definite meaning has been assigned in past ages, have now lost that meaning; and that the learned, the pious, the teachers of the nation, are incapable of discovering and fixing the sense which they are now to bear.

Let it be fairly considered how far the present state of things in this nation agrees with any of the cases above supposed: and if it does so agree, then it is maintained that, on the principle of a sacred love for truth, Subscription is become the disgrace of the English Church.

3. It cannot be argued, in mitigation of the supposed evil results, that the present controversy on this subject is confined to certain classes of society, the studious, the well-educated, the members of our Church. Half our newspapers are teeming with it; some of our periodicals are almost confined to it; all, it is believed, are occasionally employed in its discussion. It is finding its way into almost every class of society. The commercial travellers' room, we are told, has engaged in it, and much might many a sophistical controversialist learn from that numerous, acute, and ubiquitous body of men, who know more of the real opinions of the great mass of the people than any other class that can be named.

When our Lord remarked, "The harvest is plenteous," He pointed to the multitude of unconverted souls; and surely England is not without its full proportion of such, towards whom the most anxious thoughts and zealous exertions of the Christian minister are naturally to be directed. The intelligent Christian, the well-affected churchman, may be ready to make every charitable allowance for the imperfections of our Church—though charity is not the virtue of these days—but the criminal, the profligate, the sceptic, over whom it is most desirable, yet most difficult, to obtain an influence for their good, are proverbially the most acute in discerning the defects of their appointed teachers, in noting any inconsistency between the lesson and the instructor. Suspicion is the very atmosphere they breathe; and to rejoice in iniquity, especially where there is a profession of religion, is, alas! too natural and agreeable to them. In whatever degree then the teacher of truth shall expose himself to the imputation of a want of veracity amongst the irreligious, deplorable is it to contemplate the decline of a wholesome influence which must ensue. The writer has himself witnessed a lamentable instance of this result in one of the most accomplished men of late times, now no more, whom he wishes it were allowable to name. Could some of our controversialists look into a conclave of youthful profligates, led on, it may be, by some ingenious sceptic, they would blush to hear the comments on their own writings; the bitter and triumphant questions—What is it which these our discordant and subtle instructors really believe? Do they believe anything? They subscribe, and reap the profit. Let them tell us what this Subscription and these Articles of Faith really mean, and then it will be time enough for us to consider about attending to their instruction.

Add to this the obvious reasoning of the dissenting part of our population. The best amongst them cannot but see some justification of their own separation from a Church whose teachers are proclaiming throughout the land, from an hundred pens, the discordance of their sentiments as to their own Confession of Faith: not mere shades of difference reconcileable with a general agreement in its object, but a division for instance on, to them certainly, a leading question. Was the Reformation a good or an evil? The more worldly amongst them of course hail with delight what they will designate as the quibbles and evasions of men apparently eager to escape the trammels of a subscription solemnly made, which during three centuries has occasioned troubles, and persecution, and separation, and exclusion in the Christian fold, and is yet further than ever from establishing its professed purpose—"Consent touching true religion."

A still larger class, amidst the din of controversy, pick up a few popular reports which help to confirm their indifference to religion itself, and their preconceived notions as to Subscription. These people, they carelessly conclude, live by it: they wish to receive the tithes, and they must sign the Articles: now at least we know from some of themselves how much they believe them.

If these views are correct, and these apprehensions well founded, may the earnest request of one who has long pondered over these things in sadness arrest the attention of those who are capable of providing a remedy! Let not his appeal, in behalf of a Church in which he sees the elements of usefulness unparalleled, to the great body of its ministers and members whom he deeply respects, and in the cause of eternal truth, be deemed an unfriendly voice. Let him not be considered an enemy because with faithfulness, yet with humility, he entreats his countrymen to consider how far Subscription is become the disgrace of the English Church.

4. Although the present state of things as to Subscription is so notorious that it cannot be denied, yet it may be well to confirm what has been advanced by a few particulars. The Thirty-nine Articles are our Confession of Faith, though they are hardly entitled to that appellation, being drawn up rather to meet a special emergency in the history of Christianity than to present a *complete* compendium of catholic truths. Several points left untouched by them, or very briefly noticed, require at this time to be strongly inculcated. They are, however, our only Confession of Faith, ever to be valued and revered; and it is required that every clergyman should declare, and subscribe, ex animo, that he believes them to be agreeable to Scripture. A similar declaration is required with respect to the Book of Common Prayer.

It is not the writer's object to point public scorn against individuals, neither is it any satisfaction to him to notice at all the supposed defects of other men: rather is it a source of real sorrow to him to observe how censure has been cast to and fro, with an unsparing hand, by Christian writers and ministers of his own day and church. He speaks simply for the sake of truth, and in that attempt unwillingly adduces only what is necessary to his purpose. He speaks also in very general terms, considering it sufficient only to allude to opinions which unnumbered publications have rendered familiar. While the terms of our Subscription are strong and decided, several sections of the English clergy embrace a different view with respect to it.

If there be any conclusion which the history of England irresistibly conveys to readers of honest minds, it is this, that our Reformers in forty-two Articles, and afterwards in thirty-nine, intended to put forth a strong and unequivocal protest against the errors and corruptions of Romanism. Much would it have startled them to be told that the time would arrive when English clergymen would subscribe to these Articles, and then proceed to contend that they are not to be estimated as a protest against the anti-Protestant proceedings of the Council of Trent. They were accustomed, no doubt, to insincere subscription from men still Romanists at heart; but the deed was secret, it shunned the light: it was, with a very few exceptions, practised without open defence.

It is not intended to affirm that an interminable war is to be carried on by us against the Romish church: rather it is our duty to desire, without compromise, union with all Christendom. Subscription alone is now in view; and while that remains as it is, and English words retain their meaning, and an English history of facts can be found, and any clear apprehension of the meaning of truth remains with us, the perversion of our Form of Subscription, and the misrepresentation of our Articles, attempted by any who argue that they were not intended to condemn Romanism, whether as held before or after the Council of Trent, ought to excite, in every honest mind, an indignation which it is a virtue to feel, and a duty to express. If it be questioned where such views have been advanced, it is sufficient to refer to Tract No. 90, now before the writer of these pages, though other instances might be cited from authors who have subscribed the Articles.

If we turn to another section of the English clergy, that most opposed to the views of the tractarians, however they command our respect from their piety, and zeal, and hearty attachment to Scriptural truth and sound doctrine; yet some of them cannot be esteemed clear of all blame on the question now considered. The writer can here speak from personal knowledge. In their views as to baptismal regeneration, certainly opposed to the strict language of our formularies; in their dislike of other parts of our services, and sometimes in the disuse or change of certain terms, is to be found a proof that to them Subscription is not altogether satisfactory; and the often-avowed concession, that the excellence of our system of doctrine and worship, *as a whole*, reconciles their minds to some imperfections, is enough to show that, in subscribing, some violence is done to simple truth. They argue, and justly, that no human work can literally demand an unqualified approbation, but our Subscription does require it. Such arguments, then, cannot be altogether satisfactory to him who uses them, or to many to whom they may be offered; and truth, it cannot be denied, is to some extent dishonoured and damaged in their use.

In that section again of subscribers who embrace Calvinistic doctrines, though the writer considers that some of the Articles are more unequivocally favourable to them than their opponents, yet it cannot be forgotten how frequently and decidedly it has been declared, ex cathedrâ, that theirs are not the doctrines of the Church of England.

Another large section of the English clergy may be now comprised under the name of old-fashioned high-churchmen; and of that title, it is believed, they will not themselves complain. Many of them would gladly extract the honey from the tractarian school, without sufficiently considering how poisonous the plant whose growth they are to some extent fostering. They insist often on an exact compliance with Rubrics, and must forgive me for saying that few amongst them have fulfilled these in their own practice. Till very lately, it would indeed be difficult to find many clergymen, or one bishop, within the last fifty years, who have strictly observed the Rubrics—still less the Canons. Some of them speak also of a literal subscription; but here again the writer can of his own knowledge state, that numbers claim and use a considerable latitude in subscribing, and are satisfied with asserting their *general* attachment to the Formularies of the Church. Of their Arminian views as to doctrine, it is hardly necessary to call to mind how much they are opposed to others amongst their brethren, and, in the writer's judgment, to the Articles themselves.

In another section may be comprised those who desire improvement in many things relating to the spiritual affairs of our Church. Some have openly expressed this desire; a far larger number cherish it in silence. They who have spoken out have strongly stated their conviction, that a Church, without the means of even entering upon deliberation as to our general improvement in its spiritual concerns, is in a false and unscriptural position. With respect to the Forms of Subscription and the interpretation of the Articles, some have formally requested a change, or rather an authoritative solution of the many doubts and uncertainties which now embarrass the question.

Thus while we perceive the variety of opinion prevailing amongst these several sections—a variety which, were it not impeded by subscription, would find a harmless or beneficial vent in a free inquiry after Scriptural truth—we see also that from all of them, more or less, Subscription is requiring that which, in the ordinary affairs of life, high-minded men would abstain from; namely, the necessity for qualifying the plain and straight-forward use of language. Is this a condition favourable to the reputation of teachers of truth; and is it too strong a conclusion, at least from some parts of the above account, to affirm, that Subscription is the disgrace of the English Church?

5. It may be well to look at the result of such a state of things under another view. The differences above mentioned are now rendered notorious by innumerable publications. The laxity as to truth, that is with respect to the Articles, which they display, will be learnt and adopted. It will be justified by the example of clergymen who are indeed at one time censured by persons high in ecclesiastical station, yet by others in the same station applauded or defended, and never authoritatively censured or restrained. In another age a new set of opinions may arise equally differing from the literal sense of our Articles and Formularies. And who, with the precedent of these days before him, could proceed with confidence against the authors and abettors? The errors of a Socinian or an Arian may be of a more deadly character; but neither the one nor the other, in affixing his own interpretation to the Articles, or in subscribing with such doctrinal views, would depart a jot further from the true meaning of words than the author and the defenders of Tract No. 90. If that tract has driven one reader to such a conclusion, a conclusion which he states with pain and

sorrow, it may encourage hundreds to the same; and, ere long, an Arian or Socinian subscription may be as common as in times past perhaps they were, with this lamentable aggravation, that in an age of better religious feeling, "men of piety and talent," so publicly designated by Bishops of the Church, have taught the way to justify the deed.

6. The manner in which the present controversy is conducted greatly aggravates its evils. It is not only that differences exist and are eagerly discussed before the public as the judge of clerical orthodoxy, but that, owing to its character, the discussion assumes a peculiarly offensive form. It is not merely an inquiry after truth in which some warmth and zeal might be excused, but clergymen are imputing to clergymen dishonourable conduct: dishonourable on this ground, that a person holding the opinions impugned cannot be an honest subscriber, ought not to remain a minister of our Church. On all sides this discreditable course has been pursued, and it would be easy to furnish the proofs. The writer is bound frankly to own that what he condemns in others may be now charged upon himself; but never would he have entered upon these remarks except in the humble yet anxious hope that he may induce others to attempt a remedy for the evil.

Imagine such a state of things in any other profession. Imagine the Officers of the Army and Navy for years together accusing one another of dishonourably retaining their commissions. It is no answer to say that the remedy with them would be bloodshed, and that this alone restrains their pens; for this is not the fact. The accused would demand inquiry and trial, and the scandal would cease. The clergy enjoy the unenviable singularity of continuing to accuse one another, of dishonourable conduct; of acting upon mercenary motives; of a desire to make their convictions somehow square with their Subscription, that thus they may retain their position or emoluments as ministers of the Church. The controversy is disgraced throughout by an irritating reproach against character, which is neither becoming to the station of clergymen, or the manners of gentlemen; and degrades a profession which ought to be the last to exhibit such an example. It seems to be perpetually saying, such is the sense of our Confession of Faith; I have proved it, but you are subscribing in a different, in a false sense. Thus it is that Subscription, in its present state, has rendered what ought to be an inquiry after Scriptural truth, a perpetual and disgraceful taunt upon the honesty of the parties engaged. Character is damaged, or at least assailed, and no satisfactory result, no remedy ensues.

7. The circumstance last mentioned deserves consideration as another cause which, under present circumstances, helps to render our Subscription a disgrace to the English Church. Differences as to its meaning abound on all sides. Even they who uphold and would enforce a strictly literal subscription are obliged to allow of *some* latitude. Yet what is to be the

extent of this no one can say; and in the midst of all this confusion, no one attempts a remedy.

Let us turn again to the Army and Navy, and suppose their Officers discussing publicly for several years the meaning of some of the Articles of War; deluging the country with printed statements of their differences; banded into parties, each following the notions of some favoured leaders; attacking not only the sense but the honour of their opponents; professing unbounded respect for their generals, and at one moment pronouncing them almost infallible; yet the next, if they should offer an adverse opinion, combating it in no measured terms. Suppose all this, if possible, going on for years without a remedy, without a decided attempt to devise one. Once, perhaps, it was the case; and it was at last remedied, so far as he might, by the strong arm of Cromwell: but no remedy of any kind is now attempted amongst the clergy.

The Articles of War for the Army are susceptible of an annual revision, which is to be sanctioned by the Crown, and embodied in the annual Mutiny Act, and confirmed by Parliament. Those for the Navy have existed since the time of George II., but they are modified so as to meet existing views and circumstances, by "The Instructions and Regulations for Her Majesty's Service at Sea," which are altered whenever deemed advisable; and by other expedients well known to the profession. In every other profession, trade, or calling, and in every legal document relating to them, from a Royal Charter to a poor boy's indentures, we have a judge or authority competent to interpret and decide when a doubt arises. But Christians in England are either too timid or too indifferent, for wisdom it cannot be termed, to attempt an authoritative settlement of the discreditable differences and difficulties arising out of the various interpretations of their own Confession of Faith.

In assuming that this is not the path of wisdom, we have high authority. In May 1840, thirty-six clergymen, who saw the evil in its true light, and it is now immeasurably increased, signed a Petition to the House of Lords requesting attention to the subject. It was presented by His Grace the Archbishop of Dublin to a full house. Twenty-two Bishops were present. His Grace the Archbishop of Canterbury concurred in the propriety and necessity of some interpreting power. So also did the Bishops of London, and Lincoln, and Norwich, and upon this point there was no dissenting voice.

8. The present state of Subscription is also discreditable to the English Church when we consider the position in which it leaves the Bishops. Whoever wishes well to the institutions of his country, and desires to promote the peaceful happiness of the people, will watchfully cherish

respect for all who are in authority. The Christian is taught to consider them as ministers of God to us for good; and the clergy are bound, not only by this universal sanction but also by their Ordination vows, to reverence the Bishops of the Church; and any circumstance which occasions a breach in this duty ought to be to them a cause for regret.

There is a popular error that a clergyman, when in doubt upon any question of Christian faith or practice, has only to apply to his Bishop, and that he has authority to settle the question. Some recent writers have helped perhaps to foster this notion by their ill-considered professions of entire deference to episcopal authority. No circumstance has contributed so largely to expose the very limited extent of it as the controversies of the present day. A Bishop, in fact, has scarcely any discretionary power amongst the greater part of the clergy as to questions of doctrine. He can refuse ordination to a candidate, or a license to a curate, subject, however, to an appeal. If he should refuse institution to a benefice, the civil courts would demand the reason. He may institute a suit for heresy; and this must be proved by a reference to the Scriptures and four general councils, not to the Articles or Book of Prayer. Yet of late great deference to episcopal authority has been expressed, and the Charges of Bishops have been anxiously looked for. The manner in which they have been received by some exposes the hollowness of the deference professed, the absence of the power supposed, and the true reason for the anxiety to receive them. They are estimated as the works of partizans in a controversy, not of judges in a cause. They are extolled by those to whose opinions they lean; they are criticized without reserve, and sometimes with very little respect, by any who are dissatisfied with them. The truth is shown in all its nakedness, that Bishops have no more *power* on such questions than other men, and less influence perhaps than some other writers.

Yet the Bishops of the Church appear to stand somewhat in the same position as our judges. But how differently are the *dicta* of the latter received? Their decisions indeed are open to argument from their inferiors in the same profession, but before a superior court, and not by calling on the public to be the judge of written controversy between the parties. Their decisions may be reversed by a superior court, but in a solemn, respectful, and orderly manner, without being rudely assailed; and the ultimate appeal being to the House of Lords, or the Privy Council, no judge, who properly feels the liability to error in the wisest, can sustain a shock to his feelings or character if such superior tribunals should differ from his own judgment. Very different, as we have remarked, is the fate of an Episcopal Charge in these days; and, until the cause is removed, there is no prospect of remedying a state of things so discreditable to the Church: the probability is that it will be worse.

The Bishops, in fact, are endeavouring to settle that which they have not the power to settle—the meaning of Subscription, the interpretation of the Articles, the true doctrine of the Church. And whoever in a public station attempts to exercise a greater power than his office assigns, exposes a weak point perhaps before unnoticed, and instead of gaining new authority, may lose a part of that long-established and deferential respect, which is the most valuable part of all authority. A country magistrate is discreetly silent when a case is brought before him which the law does not empower him to decide, and abstains from lowering his authority by an interference which may be disputed.

It is altogether unsound in theory, and utterly fruitless in practice, to expect that points relating to doctrine can be settled by Episcopal Charges dropping one by one from the press, and unconnected with each other. The interpretation of a Confession of Faith or of the terms of Subscription belongs to the Church, in some way represented and convened. An Episcopal Charge is pastoral advice. When there is in the Church a proper authority to legislate or interpret, that advice will be received with respect and thankfulness, and contribute much in directing the minds of men to a right decision, which is its proper office. But when it usurps the province of a judge or legislator, or from circumstances is improperly brought to stand in their place, it will only provoke the opposition we now witness, and ultimately lose a part of that just deference which it ought ever to receive. The recollection that there is no Convocation or other Ecclesiastical Body competent to settle the perplexing questions recently agitated, may have induced the Bishops charitably to venture upon a forlorn hope. Their Charges however are powerless in the attempt; and however thankful numbers are to receive their pastoral advice, yet when we observe the boundless liberty of reply, and the entire want of authority to enforce their conclusions, respect for the episcopal office almost suggests the wish that in these days they were not published.

Supposing, however, the case were otherwise; suppose a real and unbounded deference to the least word of a Bishop to prevail amongst the clergy and people; suppose that they had each authority in controversies of faith; what unfortunately should we reap in the present state of things but increased perplexity? The judges—so to term them—are divided in opinion; and, though this in the parallel case of legal judges is stripped of injury by an appeal to a superior court, the Church possesses no such appeal. In the meanwhile two-thirds of our Bishops, perhaps, are ranged on one side in the present controversy, and have spoken strongly. The remainder have spoken with a leaning more or less strong in the opposite direction, or are as yet silent. As to *deciding* then the true and proper interpretation of our Articles and Subscription nothing has been gained by

Episcopal Charges. Only the unpleasing truth has been openly displayed that they may be treated like the pamphlet of any anonymous partizan. Thus the present state of the question as to Subscription operates in overthrowing respect to the office and authority of our Bishops, and this it cannot do without being discreditable to the Church.

9. They who have studied even cursorily the history of ecclesiastical affairs in England since the Reformation, may trace in Subscription another circumstance discreditable, if not disgraceful, to the English Church, and one which present times bring before our view. The most earnest and devoted section of the clergy, whatever their peculiar views in past or present times, have been frequently branded by the imputation of departing from the literal sense of the Articles, and of the Subscription required to them and the Book of Common Prayer. They have been censured also as disaffected to the Church, sometimes to its doctrines, sometimes to its rites and ceremonies. The next step has been to speak of them as unfit to remain in the ministry, and to desire their exclusion.

No candid man can doubt the piety, the ability, the zeal in their Master's service, of the puritanical divines. Yet many of them were excluded at the Restoration, and thus the Church lost a large body of Christian men, and itself laid the foundation of a considerable portion of our present non-conformity. At the end of the seventeenth century, the eminent divines who attempted to repair by healing counsels the damage thus occasioned were branded as latitudinarians, and denounced as disaffected to the Church. In the last century no attempt was made to turn into a more regular channel the zeal of Wesley and Whitfield, and their associates. They were excluded as unsound in doctrine and dangerous to true religion. With difficulty for a long time did the evangelical clergy, who sprung from them, maintain their position as a proscribed race, condemned as disaffected to the Church.

Suppose in all these cases that the charge of objecting to some parts of the Articles and Liturgy, and to the Subscription required, were true; yet to what does it amount? With these assumed errors, did not these persons believe the Bible and love it? Did they not believe all the main Articles of the Christian Faith, as taught by the Church? Was it not the earnestness of their belief which made them what they were? Were they not the very men, who, by their faith and energy, were calculated to accomplish the object of the ministry, namely, to win souls to the Redeemer's kingdom, and to form a peculiar people zealous of good works? What then was the ground of exclusion or objection? Subscription—assent to the Thirty-nine Articles and the Book of Common Prayer, according to the strict and exact terms imposed by the Church. There was not an objection, nor even indifference, to the smallest portion of the Word of God; but in some nonessential points they wished for alteration or liberty. Subscription caused the difficulty.

Whatever opinion may be now entertained of the tractarian party, the praise of zeal, ability and piety cannot be denied to the leaders of it; yet they are censured as disaffected to the Church, and their exclusion not obscurely suggested. For some of their opinions the writer can be no advocate. He believes them to have fallen into errors equally lamentable and dangerous if persisted in: yet were the choice given him between such instructors and others who pass uncondemned in ruinous indolence and indifference, he would not hesitate in giving his preference to the former. Nor, when he remembers the want of earnest men, and the ever-varying forms of human opinion, can he hesitate in desiring their continuance as ministers in our Church.

> "We are not only uncertain of finding out truths, in matters disputable, but we are certain that the best and ablest doctors of Christendom have been actually deceived in matters of great concernment; which thing is evident in all those instances of persons from whose doctrines all sorts of Christians, respectively, take liberty to dissent. The errors of Papias, Irenæus, Lactantius, Justin Martyr, in the millenary opinion; of St. Cyprian, Firmilian, the Asian and African fathers in the question of re-baptization; St. Austin in his decretory and uncharitable sentence against the unbaptized children of Christian parents; the Roman or the Greek doctors in the question of the procession of the Holy Ghost, and in the matter of images, are examples beyond exception. The errors that attach to the minds of men are numberless. Now if these great personages had been persecuted or destroyed for their opinions, who should have answered the invaluable loss the Church should have sustained in missing so excellent, so exemplary, and so great lights?"
>
> "Since those opinions were open and manifest to the world, that the Church did not condemn them, it was either because those opinions were by the Church not thought to be errors, or if they were, yet she thought fit to tolerate the error and the erring person. And if she would do so still, it would, in most cases, be better than now it is."—*Bishop Jeremy Taylor.*

In our own case, what would be gained by the exclusion of the persons just referred to? The past may teach us that this will not silence men earnest in their convictions, or promote the unity we desire. But, if their opinions are to be tolerated within the ministry of our Church, then, in common justice, and for the credit of that Church, the stigma ought to be removed which now attaches to them as insincere subscribers. It is this which makes the present controversy so bitter and disingenuous. Remove the irritation occasioned by this perpetual taunt, and is there not ground to hope that it would settle down into an unfettered inquiry after Scriptural truth, and that the result would be a more universal deference to the Word of God? Such is the trust which the writer cannot but entertain.

To wait charitably in patience and hope on the one hand; and on the other to concede all that can be conceded without compromise of truth, for union and unity, are Christian duties; but it is not the dictate of wisdom or charity to repel hastily from the ministry, zeal and piety which cannot be spared, and which the providence of God may eventually overrule and direct to the great good of the people. And if Subscription involves us in the danger of repeatedly excluding the most zealous portion of our clergy, it is a disgrace to the Church which continues to enforce it.

10. About two years ago the writer ventured to name a remedy for the evils and inconveniences arising out of the embarrassed state of the Subscription now required. His proposal was, that a clergyman should subscribe to the Three Creeds, instead of the Articles and Liturgy, retaining the other tests or pledges now in use. Within the last twelve months he has had the satisfaction of observing, that, on an occasion of great interest to Christians in this and other nations, a plan very closely resembling this, as he understands it, has been adopted under the sanction of the highest ecclesiastical authority. On the appointment of an English Bishop for Jerusalem, which was effected, as is well known, in conjunction with His Majesty the King of Prussia, it was determined to make such regulations that the subjects of that King, employed either as missionaries or ministers of congregations in Palestine, might receive the full benefit of episcopal sanction and superintendence. This was effected in the manner described by the following Letters, which appeared in the Prussian *State Gazette* of July 12th, 1842.

> THE BISHOPRIC OF JERUSALEM.
>
> Berlin, July 11.
>
> His Majesty has been pleased to address to the minister of Ecclesiastical Affairs the following orders in respect to the relations of the Bishop of the United Church of England and Ireland in Jerusalem with the German congregation of the evangelical religion in Palestine:—

"I send you herewith a letter from his Grace the Archbishop of Canterbury, Primate of England, which contains the definitive proposals respecting the relations of the Bishop of the United Church of England and Ireland in Jerusalem with the German congregations of the evangelical religion in Palestine, which are inclined to place themselves under the jurisdiction of the latter. You will see from this letter that the Prelate secures to the congregations of the German Protestant faith in Palestine the protection and pastoral care of the English Bishop at Jerusalem, without any other conditions than such as the exercise of the protection itself requires. The publication of these proposals will be the best means to dispel the misunderstanding of some well-meaning persons, and to render the misrepresentations and calumnies of the evil-minded of no effect. Though there are at present no German Protestant congregations in Palestine, but the formation is still to be looked for under the influence of favourable circumstances, yet young divines of the German Protestant Church, whom the increasing interest in the labours of the missions for the conversion of the Jews induces to go to Palestine, will certainly think it desirable to avail themselves of the offers contained in the letter of the Archbishop of Canterbury, to obtain a greater freedom of action and a more successful result of their labours, by accepting the protection and care of the Bishop of the United Church of England and Ireland. I am very ready to support, in a suitable manner, young divines of this kind, when they have been examined and found duly qualified, and especially proved themselves to be thoroughly grounded in the doctrines of the Protestant faith, according to the Augsburg Confession, and I invite you to point out to me any such persons.

"Frederick William.

"To the Minister of State, Eichhorn."

"Lambeth, June 18, 1842.

"Sire,—As it seems to me to be desirable that your Majesty should be thoroughly acquainted with the relations in which the German congregations in Palestine will stand with respect to the Bishop of the United Church of England and Ireland in Jerusalem, I take the liberty most respectfully to submit the following proposals, which I hope will be agreeable to your Majesty:—

"The Bishop will consider it as his duty to take under his pastoral care and protection all the congregations of the German Protestant faith which are within the limits of his diocese, and are inclined to place themselves under his jurisdiction, and will afford them all the support in his power. The German Liturgy, which has been carefully examined by me, which is taken from the liturgies received in the churches of your Majesty's dominions, will be used in the celebration of divine service by the clergymen who are appointed, on the following principle:—Young divines, candidates for the pastoral office in the German Church, who have obtained your Majesty's Royal permission to this end, will exhibit to the Bishop a certificate from some authority appointed by your Majesty, in which their good conduct as well as their qualification for the pastoral office is in every respect attested. The Bishop will, of course, take care, in the case of every candidate so presented to him, to convince himself of his qualifications for the especial duties of his office, of the purity of his faith, and of his desire to receive ordination from the hands of the Bishop. As soon as the Bishop has fully satisfied himself on these points, he will ordain the candidate on his subscribing the three Creeds, the Apostles', the Nicene, and the Athanasian, and, on his taking the oath of obedience to the Bishop and his successor, will give him permission to exercise the functions of his office.

"With respect to the confirmation of young persons of such congregations in Palestine, the Clergyman of the congregation will prepare them for that purpose in the usual manner, will subject them to the requisite examination, and receive from them, in the presence of the congregation, the profession of their faith. They will then be presented to the Bishop, who will confirm them according to the form of the Liturgy of the United Church of England and Ireland.

"With the most profound respect,

"I have the honour to remain,
Sire,

"Your Majesty's most sincere and humble Servant,

"W. Canterbury.

"To his Majesty Frederick William IV.,
　　　　King of Prussia."

It is of course impossible to suppose that such a step was taken without much deliberation: and here we see, first, that an English Bishop, regularly consecrated by the Archbishop of Canterbury and other Bishops at Lambeth, is authorised to confer Holy Orders, requiring from the persons ordained Subscription to the Three Creeds only.

When it is remembered how long the Christian Church has been divided and rent, and how the Protestant part of it is again subdivided into numerous sections, sometimes in the same nation, any approach towards the establishment of a sound and primitive catholic test, which may enable a larger number of Christians to enjoy communion with one another, ought to be viewed with thankfulness. More especially ought it to be so viewed by ourselves, if there be a hope that the example can be adopted as the means of promoting peace amongst the ministers and members of the *same Church*—namely, our own—now so unhappily disunited; and if the great Truths in which they *agree* could be thus prominently exhibited to the world. And, if the rule laid down with reference to our Christian brethren of the Prussian Church be sound and judicious; if it has been wisely and charitably selected as calculated to unite many who have hitherto been separated in communion, though not materially in doctrine; why should it not be applied to secure similar advantages amongst Englishmen, and to heal some of the wounds which are daily inflicted on the peace of the Church by its own ministers and members?

Let not such a proposal be hastily rejected from an unexamined apprehension that the doctrines of the Reformation are to be surrendered. Let it at least be calmly and candidly considered. The remarks hitherto offered may be disputed as incorrect; but no one can possibly deny that the state of the English Church is unsatisfactory, perhaps unsafe. The writer can in all sincerity declare himself, in the fullest sense of the word, a Protestant: yet he may, very consistently, with such a declaration, desire to see Protestants Catholics, and in fulfilment of the pledge given at ordination "to maintain and set forwards, as much as in him lieth, quietness, and peace, and love, among all Christian people." These are what the Universal Church now requires for her prosperity and success.

While the above-named catholic test was adopted to meet the peculiar situation and duties of the new Bishop in Jerusalem, we see that it was at the same time provided that candidates for ordination, subjects of the King of Prussia, should be examined generally as to their qualifications for the ministry; and also as to their being thoroughly grounded in the Augsburg Confession, the foundation of our Articles; and further, that a certificate of their having satisfactorily passed such an examination should be laid before the Bishop of Jerusalem, who will also take care to convince himself of their fitness to receive ordination at his hands.

If we were to transfer this whole precedent, as the writer understands it, to our own Church, the change it would make would be simply this, namely, that it would be left to the Bishops, each exercising the discretionary power now vested in him, to judge, upon examination, of the doctrinal views of a candidate, instead of requiring him to subscribe to the Thirty-nine Articles. And if we draw this out into practice, the loss as to security for any particular doctrines would be none. Each Bishop would of course exercise the discretionary power as he now does, and the same candidates would be admitted; but the evils now attending upon Subscription would be remedied, or immeasurably diminished.

A candidate would be examined as to his general qualifications, and also by questions on the Thirty-nine Articles, according to the judgment of each Bishop, and might be received or rejected, as is now the case. Whatever point in the Articles might appear to each Bishop to require particular attention would be made a subject of examination, as is now the case. Any question relative to doctrinal views, deemed necessary, might be put, and the Bishop would have the actual view of the candidate in his own words; and, if his word will not bind a man, will his signature? If a candidate, for instance, professed that he considered the Reformation injurious or imperfect, the Bishop might reject him, or not; and if he did not profess this, but afterwards came to that opinion, the case would only be as it is sometimes now. Possibly Bishops might differ as to their mode of conducting such examination; and in one diocese a candidate might be received who might fear being rejected in another; for so it has been, and may be again; and thus persons of various shades of opinion are admitted to the ministry, probably to the benefit of the Church.

After examination, and previous to ordination, each candidate would subscribe to the Three Creeds, [33] and engage to conform to the Liturgy. At his ordination, as a priest, he would promise before the congregation to study the Word of God, to teach nothing contrary to it, and to fulfil the duties of the ministry according to the solemn and comprehensive pledges of our Ordination Service, to which the writer requests a particular attention in connection with this subject. There is here no want of security so far as pledges can give it; and every advantage *really secured* on the present plan would be retained. The present Subscription does not produce consent touching true religion, whereas an assent to the doctrine of the

Creeds would be almost catholic. The present Subscription does not secure attachment to the doctrines of the Reformation. What advantage then does it realize which would be lost on the plan proposed? They who love the Reformation and revere our Articles, would love and revere them still. It is not Subscription which draws forth their attachment, but conviction—the conviction that they are founded on the Word of God, coupled with a thankful recollection of the men and the times which gave them to us.

Let it not be forgotten that, whatever power the laws now give for restraining or punishing those who impugn the Articles or Liturgy, would remain untouched. And in all cases where the law does speak, it ought to be the test of wrong doing. So long as it was not called forth, the just presumption would be that no such offence had been committed; and controversy, which must always exist while truth is loved, would be carried on without the discreditable concomitants detailed above.

The precedent adopted then, on the appointment of a Bishop for Jerusalem, suggests an unobjectionable improvement; [34] and it carries with it this further recommendation that it would bring the law and the practice together, which is always considered sound legislation when the practice has become so established that the law is virtually repealed. Instances of this kind are well known. The repeal of the Corporation and Test Acts was little more than a formal abrogation of a law no longer in force; and the repeal of the present form of Subscription would, in like manner, only legally confirm that latitude of interpretation with respect to it which already prevails. [35]

11. If, however, the above-named precedent be rejected, there are yet unquestionable grounds for desiring that something should be done in the present state of things. It is asked, not in a hostile or unreasonable spirit, but seriously, soberly, and earnestly—for the peace of the Church; for the credit of its ministers and members; and for the sake of truth itself—that we may be told in what sense Subscription may be, or ought to be, made. It has been of late advanced as an argument against those who would set up various human authorities as arbiters of truth; that the Church has already declared the truth by her interpretation of Scripture, that she has given us that interpretation in our Thirty-nine Articles, and bound it upon us by Subscription. We answer simply, that the interpretation itself is disputed, that the sense of it cannot be fixed. We want, therefore, a new decision.

It has been argued again that Subscription preserves truth within the Church. We simply ask, *what* truth? and affirm that the constant use of our Liturgy preserves pure doctrine more effectually, and always will. It has been advanced also, somewhat inconsiderately, but by high authority, as an argument against alteration, that any change might make matters worse, by making Subscription more strict. We answer that, if it requires an assent to that which is scripturally true, it cannot be too strict. Let it then be strictly and literally enforced: but, if this be deemed unadvisable or impossible, let it be interpreted anew, or repealed. In its present state it cannot be too plainly or repeatedly affirmed, that it is a disgrace to the Church.

12. It may be pronounced absurd or presumptuous in an individual to propose a change in such a matter as Subscription to Articles of Faith, but in truth *a great change has already taken place*. There have been in past ages considerable variations as to doctrinal views prevailing at different times: of late a new character has been given to Subscription; new certainly to this generation, and new altogether, as proceeding from persons remaining in the ministry; for the principal abettors of similar views in past times are found amongst the non-jurors, and were seceders from the establishment. A few years ago it was pronounced by a Bishop to be little less than a libel on the Church, to say that the clergy did not subscribe literally to the Articles. Since that time another Bishop has designated a system of interpretation put forth and defended by clergymen, as "so subtle, that by it the Articles may be made to mean any thing or nothing." Several episcopal charges have spoken to the same effect, and almost innumerable publications from other authors. Yet the principles on which that system is founded, are disseminated with unabated zeal and increased influence. The Tracts for the Times, silenced only by name, are issued in reviews, magazines, pamphlets, poems, and novels; and the same views as to the Reformation and the Articles are maintained, though the application of them, in the manner proposed by Tract No. 90, may be partially disowned. A *great change then has taken place*; and the result is, that Subscription has received a blow from which it can never recover without some decided measure. It must become an object of general ridicule or contempt, of which, indeed, some indications have already appeared.

To this the writer desires to invite attention. If he has ventured to propose a remedy, it is principally on this ground, that whoever points out a defect in existing institutions is commonly asked, what improvement can you offer? Although, then, convinced that the remedy he has named is calculated to meet the evil, it is rather his wish that others should be induced to come forward, and so to deal with the change which has taken place that it may cease to be a reproach to the Church. With this object before him, he believes himself engaged in the cause of truth, and will continue to devote to it the limited powers he possesses while life is spared. And let it not be deemed presumptuous if, under an humiliating sense of his own insufficiency, he yet perseveres in recommending what is so far beyond his power to accomplish. No one can reasonably expect visible success in any undertaking. It is enough to enjoy the assurance that we are persevering in a right path. The result may well be left to the Supreme Disposer of all things. Nor are instruments in His hands weak, as man estimates power; but the weakest may be permitted to sow the seed destined to bring forth much fruit. It is the progress of conviction wrought in the minds of men which prepares the way for improvements. It is the open statement of these convictions, here and there, which leads to action.

Few improvements, if any, in the moral world can be novelties. They are only a return to some good old principle which the great innovator, time, or rather the great deteriorator, human corruption, hath thrown into the shade. An age there was, perhaps a better than this, when human Articles were unknown to the Church; an age also when the shortest of our Creeds sufficiently expressed the faith of a believer. It does not require learning or talent to state all this, and to beg others to recollect that, if heresies call for Articles, a folio would scarcely suffice. Simple minds may state such simple truths, and God may cause their voice to be heard.

Nor can it be justly affirmed that, to expose even in strong terms prevailing defects, is any proof of disaffection to the Church in which they exist. The writers of Scripture, although Divinely inspired, are yet a pattern to their less favoured followers. And who can peruse the writings of the Prophets and Apostles without being struck by their bold and uncompromising denunciations of the sins and errors prevailing amongst high and low, learned and ignorant, teachers and people? If it be disaffection to the Church, to describe faithfully and plainly an evil which requires a remedy, then is Isaiah to be condemned in his first chapter, and St. Paul in his most celebrated Epistles, instead of being our examples and instructors in the path of ministerial duty.

If the remarks above offered be well founded, they cannot be a matter of indifference, for they affect all to whom truth, and religion, and the credit of its ministers, and the national honour are dear: and all such might, without compromise of any principle or opinion, as the writer believes, join in an address to the following effect:—

> To Her Most Gracious Majesty Queen Victoria, over all persons and in all causes Ecclesiastical and Temporal within Her Dominions supreme.
>
> We your Majesty's faithful subjects have observed with pain the Controversies now for some time carried on with respect to the true interpretation of the Thirty-nine Articles of Religion and of the Subscription by law required to them and to the Book of Common Prayer; and we humbly pray your Majesty to institute such measures as to your wisdom shall seem fit, with the advice of your

Majesty's Privy Council, in order to provide a remedy for the uncertainty prevailing upon this subject.

IT is with reluctance that I add to the above remarks any that relate merely to myself. Some circumstances, however, appear to require a few brief observations.

In a former publication on the Meaning of Subscription, [41] occasioned by the extreme uncertainty and perplexity in which this subject is involved, I stated my readiness to resign my preferment, if called upon to do so within a certain time by His Grace the Archbishop of Canterbury. That call has not been made. It may, however, be supposed that the remarks now offered on the same subject are published, not so much with a view to any general improvement as from a desire to obtain relief for my own difficulties. I wish therefore distinctly to state that this is not the case, and that those difficulties are removed, for the present, on the following grounds.

Within the last three years a departure from the plain and obvious meaning of the Articles has been displayed, to an unparalleled extent, amongst the ministers of our Church; yet no call has been authoritatively made upon any of them to resign, and they retain their situations, with the exception of two or three who have voluntarily seceded. In this state of things, I can hardly imagine any diversity of opinion with respect to the Thirty-nine Articles which calls for the resignation of a clergyman; indeed, it appears to me that it would be simply absurd in any one to resort to such a step, unless under a decided wish for communion with some other church or body of Christians.

It can hardly be necessary to say, after what has been already offered, how far I am from desiring that such a state of things should continue, however unfavourably a change might affect myself: for I still maintain,—

That the condemnatory clauses of the Athanasian Creed, in their literal sense, are an un-Christian appendage to a document of extraordinary merit, yet such that a true Christian may innocently differ from some propositions set forth in it.

That a Bishop is not authorized by the Gospel to address a candidate for Ordination in the literal sense of the words, "Receive the Holy Ghost: whose sins thou dost remit, they are remitted, and whose sins thou dost retain, they are retained."

That a Christian minister is not authorized by the Gospel to address any one in the literal sense of the words, "I absolve thee from all thy sins."

Entertaining these views, I yet venture to conclude that I could subscribe the Articles and Liturgy with as near an approach to a literal assent as most of the clergy, and certainly with a far more cordial approbation of them than many who might be named. It has been said that the objections just mentioned are trifling. Whoever has marked the course of the controversy now existing in our Church will see how great a stress has been sometimes laid on two of the above points, as materially supporting the views of tractarian writers.

I have now only to acknowledge the comments of several clergymen and others in this diocese upon my last publication. To the Rev. B. Philpot, formerly Archdeacon of the Isle of Man, and to the Rev. C. Green, Rector of Burgh, I beg to offer my sincere thanks for the candid and Christian spirit in which their observations were made. I avail myself also of this opportunity to acknowledge with respect and gratitude a large number of private communications, both from friends and strangers, which were a valuable testimony at a period when they were most acceptable.

There are a few whom I have also to thank for having placed before me every fault in my conduct, and every objection to my statements, which, I conclude, from the tenour of their remarks, could be discovered or supposed. It is related, I think, of Archbishop Tillotson that he had in a conspicuous part of his library a collection of remarkably bound books; and that, on a friend inquiring what they were, he answered, "Those are my best friends—the authors who have written against me." With the same feeling, I beg again to thank the writers last mentioned; though I must express my regret that Christians should write in a spirit so unbecoming, according to my view, in a true follower of the Gospel of Christ.

THE END.

FOOTNOTES.

[33] In proposing this test, it is assumed that the view of the late Professor of Divinity, Bishop Marsh, with regard to the condemnatory clauses attached to the Athanasian Creed, would be thenceforward considered as established in our Church. His words are, "I do not mean to defend those anathemas. They are no part of the Creed itself."

[34] The establishment of such a test in our own Church might materially assist, as an example, in securing a great collateral benefit. They who are interested in missionary exertions know how great an impediment to their success arises from the differences and divisions amongst the ministers sent forth from various churches and societies. One mischievous effect of these is, that the general consent *which really exists* as to catholic truths is *obscured*. The differences on other points are always on the surface. Thus they command an undue degree of attention and importance; and, not to mention other evils, the conclusion must occur to unbelievers, that no one certain system of truth can be collected from that which is proposed to them as a Divine Revelation.

To separate the points of difference from the common bond of union, by affixing some *decided* mark of preference and distinction on the latter, would be something gained in attempts to evangelize the world. It might be better still, if one Creed, the Nicene, were chosen as the test. A very large proportion of Christian missionaries, it is presumed, would cordially bear testimony to its truth. Thus it would present some common bond of union amongst them in "preaching the Gospel to all nations"—an imperfect one, it may be said, yet apparently the best which can be secured. For almost every doctrinal point beyond that Creed is controverted; and, at the end of eighteen centuries, every church must be content to see its distinctive claims to reception rest on argument rather than authority.

[35] Private opinion, or judgment, it is very clear, cannot be controlled by Subscription, or by any other means; yet peace might be preserved, to a great extent, if the Church had the power to enjoin silence on any particular point amongst its ministers. In some respects it would be dangerous to grant such a power; but the wisest human arrangements are frequently only *choosing the least of two evils*.

The recent sentence on Dr. Pusey may be very proper as regards the religious instruction offered to students at an university, but will of course decide nothing as to the general controversy.

Only the voice of the Church can effect this, and it is time that the Church should at least *be able* to speak, though its first decision might endanger the existence of the *Establishment*. Faith, however, is a better counsellor than Fear.

[41] "What is the Meaning of Subscription?" Longmans. 1841.